GOLF
Tee'd Off

THE BEST GOLFER'S EXCUSES, QUOTES & JOKES

The ultimate gift for golfers who have everything! This funny golf book is perfect for golfers who appreciate a good laugh on and off the course, even if it's at their own expense.

A comical collection of the best, most absurd, and relatable golfer's excuses ever heard or used on the green and fairway. Professionally illustrated and filled with witty and sometimes corny one-liners, jokes, excuses, anecdotes and inspirational quotes from some of the best golf players in the world.

There's an excuse to justify every wayward shot, slice, hook, topped ball, missed putt and general frustration of the game we all love. Throw in some golfer's gags and tales from golf's greatest and you have the perfect manual to rationalise every eventuality.

Written for anyone who is passionate about their long and short game, even if the flair and finesse is sometimes lacking. It's more than just another golf book; it's a shared love of golf humour that only the frustrated golfer and anyone unlucky enough to listen to them can appreciate.

"My putter's grip is giving up the ghost; it feels like I'm trying to hold onto a wet bar of soap on every putt."

Golfer's *Excuse*

"I knew I had the wrong club."

"That gust of wind put me off."

"What a terrible lie!"

"My foot slipped!"

"I've lost my lucky ball marker, and now I'm out here feeling like I'm missing my secret weapon."

"Bad bounce."

"The tee markers are literally pointing the wrong way!"

"**G**olf is a compromise between what your ego wants you to do, what experience tells you to do, and what your nerves let you do."
Bruce Crampton (Golf's original Ironman – famed for his long-playing schedules)

The higher a golfer's handicap is, the higher the probability is they'll offer advice on how to improve your game.

"You're so absorbed in golf that it makes me wonder, do you even recall our wedding day?"
"Certainly! It's etched in my memory—the day I flawlessly nailed a 30-foot putt."

"A day where I don't golf might not be fatal, but who wants to take that chance?"

Two golfers stand poised to drive off from the 8th tee as a funeral procession moves past. Pausing his preparations, the first player tips his cap and places his arm across his chest in a gesture of respect.

Observing the act, the second golfer remarks, "That was a thoughtful gesture. It's reassuring to witness such signs of respect these days."

"It's only fitting", the first golfer responds. "After all, I shared 28 years of marriage with her."

"**T**he only thing a golfer needs is more daylight."
Ben Hogan (Post WWII golf legend)

Golfer's *Excuses*

"I haven't played for ages."

"I don't know what's happening; I've been driving great recently."

"Too windy"

"The ball is muddy"

"Didn't follow through."

"The sun was in my eyes."

"I put a little too much muscle into that swing and ended up excavating more turf than I intended."

Golfer's *Excuse*

"The greens were rubbish"

When our putting game doesn't mirror Jordan Spieth's, we often blame the greens. There's always a handful of putts that seemed absolutely destined for success but suddenly veer off course at the last second.

Or if it's not that it's sure to be the slower pace of the putting green compared to the course. How many times have you heard someone moaning about how it took them a solid 9-12 holes to grasp the speed of the greens?

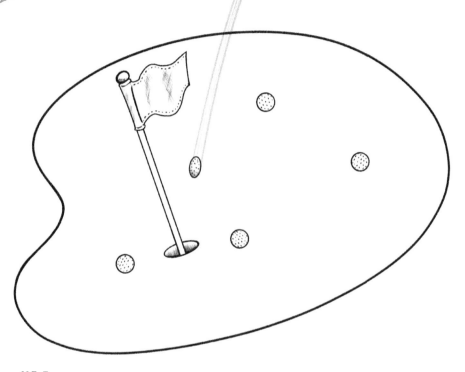

"**H**itting a golf ball and putting have nothing in common. They're two different games. You work all your life to perfect a repeating swing that will get you to the greens, and then you have to try to do something that is totally unrelated. There shouldn't be any cups, just flag sticks. And then the man who hits the most fairways and greens and got closest to the pins would be the tournament winner."
Ben Hogan (Golf legend and WWII hero)

The world of golf can often be baffling when it comes to numbers. They hit a "6," shout "fore," and end up recording a "5".

What's the biggest difference you'd find between a golfer and a skydiver? A skydiver has ten times more chance of landing on the green.

Stuart and David are enjoying a great round of golf when Stuart, teeing off the 4th, unfortunately drives his ball into a densely wooded area on the perimeter of the fairway. Without a second thought he grabs hold of his 6-iron and scrambles down the embankment in search of his lost ball.

Navigating through thick trees, his search leads him to a surprising discovery – a shiny 6-iron clutched by a skeleton next to a decaying golf ball. Anxiously, he calls out to his golfing companion, David, beckoning him to join.

David rushes to the edge of the wood, concerned, and asks, "What's going on, Stu? Are you okay?"

Stuart shouts back, "I've stumbled upon a bit of a predicament down here. Throw me my 7-iron! There's no chance of getting out of here with a six!

"**I** look into eyes, shake their hand, pat their back, and wish them luck, but I am thinking, I am going to bury you."
SEVE BALLESTEROS (Five time Ryder cup team winner)

"I seem to struggle with putting on these greens."

Here's a fresh take on this excuse: it's not about the greens! There's a common tendency to blame the condition of the greens for poor putting skills. "I only managed 24 points – the greens were in terrible shape!" However, it's improbable that a round with a subpar score is a result of flawlessly hitting every fairway and green, only to be thwarted by the putting surface. It's time to own up to the short-game challenges and focus on improving those putting skills.

Golfer's *Excuse*

"A fly flew in my ear."

"Someone moved."

"I went a bit overboard with the hip rotation on that shot."

"Haven't played in weeks."

"I play for the exercise, not the score."

"My rangefinder must be faulty."

"My hands were sweaty."

"That was just a practice swing."

Golfer's *Wisdom*

"**J**esus Christ can't hit a golf ball straight. It's
virtually impossible - at best it's an accident."
Ben Hogan (Golf legend and WWII hero)

What is it about golf that can turn a man into a toddler...how can an intelligent adult suddenly lose their ability to count past 5?

Golf balls share many similarities with eggs—they're white, come in boxes of 12 and pretty soon you're back at the shop to get more.

Ever noticed that golf commentators all seem to whisper their words?
It's because they're being considerate to the sleeping audience.

At the golf club, Jimmy and Brian were known for their intense rivalry, especially when it came to scorekeeping. Suspicion lingered between them during every game. One day, in the midst of a heated round, they eyed each other closely. After completing the fourth green and noting down his score of 5, Jimmy turned to Brian and asked, "How'd you do?"

Brian went through the mental motions of tallying his score. "5!" he declared, then quickly corrected himself, "No, actually... a 4."

Remaining composed, Jimmy recorded the scores, calmly stating, "7!" Perplexed, Brian responded, "7? How do you figure that?"

Jimmy explained, "You initially claimed 5, then changed to 4, but in reality, you had 6."

Puzzled, Brian questioned, "Then why mark down 7?"

With a sly grin, Jimmy replied, "One stroke penalty, my friend, for improving your lie."

"**I**t's good sportsmanship to not pick up lost golf balls while they are still rolling."
Mark Twain (American writer & humourist)

"I need to replace this grip."

"Didn't eat breakfast."

"Didn't warm up."

"The grass is far too long here."

"My back is giving me terrible trouble at the moment."

"My jacket is tight."

"I can't believe I sliced it. I never slice it."

"Too much noise put me off!"

"The ground isn't level."

"You were standing in the wrong place!"

"The holes seem too small."

"The gust of wind knocked my ball offline."

"That was a really unlucky bounce."

Was it? Or was it the fact that you hit it in the direction of the lake in the first place?

Perhaps if your aim was a little more accurate and less afforded to Lady-Luck then the unfortunate kick wouldn't have cost you so dearly!

The truth is a poor round isn't a result of a bad bounce but a shoddy shot.

Golfer's Anecdote

"**A**ggressive play is a vital asset of the world's greatest golfers. However, it's even more important to the average player. Attack this game in a bold, confident, and determined way and you'll make a giant leap toward realising your full potential as a player."

Greg Norman (Golf's very own 'Great White Shark')

Standing in the driving rain one cold morning a new golfer turns to his experienced partner to ask "Is it ever too wet to play golf do you think?"

"Never" replies the man..."unless your cart capsizes."

THE LONG GAME
Golfer's *Gag*

Joseph and Noah decide to squeeze in a quick 9-hole round of golf before dinner. To add a bit of excitement, Joseph proposes a friendly wager of £10 on the player with the lowest score.

As the game progresses, they reach the 8th hole, with Noah leading by one stroke. However, things take a turn on the 9th hole when Noah makes a slice, and his ball disappears in the rough. Facing the challenge, Noah asks Joseph for help locating his lost ball.

Frustrated, Noah cannot locate it and, aware of the two-stroke penalty for a lost ball, he slyly pulls a spare from his trouser pocket and throws it to the ground, jubilantly declaring, "Found it!"

Baffled, Joseph looks at him and remarks, "After all these years of friendship, you'd resort to cheating for a measly £10?"

Trying to look hurt, Noah defends himself, saying, "What do you mean? My ball is right here!"

Joseph indignantly retorts, "And you're a bloody liar too! For the past five minutes, I've been keeping your ball hidden with my foot!"

"**I**f you watch a game, it's fun. If you play it, it's recreation. If you work at it, it's golf."
Bob Hope (Entertainer and golf enthusiast)

Golfer's *Excuse*

"That's unusual; my drive is normally great."

An all-time classic excuse is to give the impression that a poor game is a rare off-day! Continually feigning bewilderment and fake frustration after every missed fairway to underline that this is an incredibly unusual and unlikely turn of events when, in reality, it's a common occurrence.

Golfer's *Excuse*

"The course was too crowded."

"My sunglasses were scratched."

"Fairways were too narrow."

"The greens were way too slow."

"Too hot"

"Too cold"

Golfer's *Anecdote*

"**O**ne of the most fascinating things about golf is how it reflects the cycle of life. No matter what you shoot – the next day you have to go back to the first tee and begin all over again and make yourself into something."
Peter Jacobsen (Charismatic golfer, commentator & course designer)

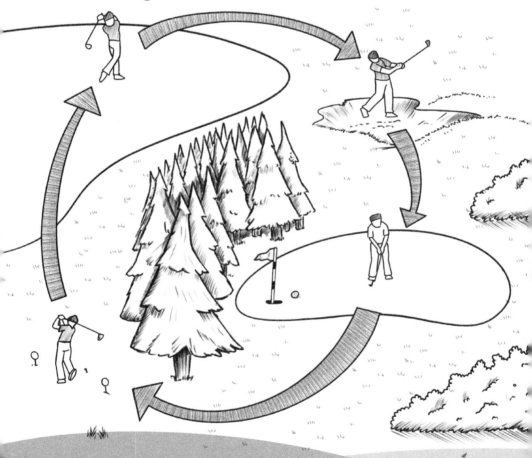

Why is it that when playing a round of golf, those ahead of you are the slowest, yet those behind suddenly become the fastest?

Golf seems like a divine creation intended to penalise those who choose early retirement.

Enhancing your golf skills can be achieved only through tuition, relentless practice, or, as a last resort, deceit.

Definition of golf: a four mile walk full of frustrations.

Robert and his wife Susan walk into a dentist's office in a hurry. Robert hastily addresses the dentist, "Listen, I'm in quite a rush. I've got two pals waiting in my car for us all to play golf. Skip the anaesthetic; I don't have time for everything to get numb. Just pull out the tooth, and let's get it over with!"

The dentist, intrigued by Robert's urgency, thinks to himself, "Wow, this is one brave fella asking for a tooth extraction without any pain relief." So, the dentist inquires, "Which tooth is bothering you?"

Robert turns to his wife and tells her, "Open your mouth babe and show him..."

"**A** golf ball is like a clock. Always hit it at 6 o'clock and make it go toward 12 o'clock. But make sure you're in the same time zone."
Chi Chi Rodriguez (Eight time PGA winner famous for his shot-making)

"The ball was in a divot."

"The ball hooked."

"My putts broke the wrong way."

"The air feels very heavy."

"The greens are too small."

"I kept looking up."

"The rough was too rough."

Golfer's *Anecdote*

"**N**o other game combines the wonder of nature with the discipline of sport in such carefully planned ways. A great golf course both frees and challenges a golfer's mind."
Tom Watson (Winner of eight major championships)

Golfer's *Anecdote*

"**G**olf cannot be played in anger, or in any mood of emotional excess. Half the golf balls struck by amateurs are hit, if not in rage, surely in bewilderment, or gloom, or in cynicism, or even hysterically - all of those emotional excesses must be contained by the professional. Which is why balance is one of the essential ingredients of golf. Professionals invariably trudge phlegmatically around the course - whatever emotions are seething within - with the grim yet placid and bored look of cowpokes, slack-bodied in their saddles, who have been tending the same herd for two months."

George Plimpton (Renowned sports journalist)

The club-wielding cavemen who roared and smashed their clubs to the grounds are often thought to be the ancestors of the modern golfer.

As a general guideline ...if your opponent can't remember if it was a six or seven he shot... then you know it was definitely an eight.

A dedicated but somewhat inexperienced female golfer took enthusiastic swings at the golf ball, causing great divots of turf to scatter in every direction.

"Oh dear," she remarked to her caddie, embarrassed, "the worms might mistake this for an earthquake."

Winking to her, the caddie replied, "I don't think so. The worms around here are pretty smart. They'll all be jostling for position right underneath the ball as we speak."

"**A**fter all these years, it's still embarrassing for me to play on the American golf tour. Like the time I asked my caddie for a sand wedge and he came back ten minutes later with a ham on rye."
Chi Chi Rodriguez (Eight time PGA winner famous for his shot-making)

Golfer's *Anecdote*

"**Y**ou don't have the game you played last year or last week. You only have today's game. It may be far from your best, but that's all you've got. Harden your heart and make the best of it."
Walter Hagen (Three time Claret Jug winner)

Golfer's *Excuse*

"The dog chewed my golf shoes."

"I think I slept on my shoulder funny. It's affecting my swing."

"I looked up by mistake."

"The tee was leaning too far forward."

"I got nervous for some reason then, just when I was swinging."

"I'm struggling to find my usual sweet spot today."

"**A**ddressing a golf ball would seem to be a simple matter; that is, to the uninitiated who cannot appreciate that a golf ball can hold more terrors than a spacious auditorium packed with people."
Bobby Jones (World Golf Hall of Fame inductee)

Never let anyone tell you that golf is a rich man's sport. It's just not true, there are literally millions of poor players everywhere you look.

Golf shares common ground with your bank balance; you aim for the green but often find yourself in the hole.

It's not that I missed the putt; the ball simply decided to avoid the hole.

Golf enthusiasts are known for their healthy eating habits, indulging in greens as much as they can.

Golfer's *Gag*

Observing that her husband looked more irritated than usual after his Sunday game of golf, his wife asked, "What's the matter with you?"

He answered, "We're only at the 3rd hole when Alex grabs his chest, falls to the floor, has a heart attack and dies right there on the green. It was truly dreadful! The remaining part of the round felt like a surreal nightmare. As well as carrying my clubs, I had to drag Alex for the remaining 15 holes. Unbearable!"

"**G**olf is a game whose aim is to hit a very small ball into an ever-smaller hole, with weapons singularly ill-designed for the purpose."
Winston Churchill (Inspirational war-time British Prime Minister)

"I've learned my lesson - no more experimenting with the cross-handed putter grip for me."

"I squandered my perfect shot during a warm-up swing."

"I mistakenly believed I had grabbed a different club for that swing."

"My handicap? Well, I operate on the "one mulligan per hole" system."

"My swagger got the best of me after my previous successful round."

"I think the ball has lost its shape."

Golf can be aptly described as an unending series of setbacks with an occasional stroke of luck.

For some golfers, the most challenging aspect is mastering the skill of accurate arithmetic.

"**G**olf is the closest game to the game we call life. You get bad breaks from good shots; you get good breaks from bad shots - but you have to play the ball where it lies."
Bobby Jones (World Golf Hall of Fame inductee)

"The tint on the lenses on these sunglasses is throwing me off."

"My ball hugged the cart path too tight, and now it's rolling on the green like it's on a bumpy road."

"The tee area is in rough shape; I can't get a clean setup."

"This morning dew is causing me problems."

Golfer's *Excuse*

"These clubs are proving tricky to get the hang of!"

There's always that one player cycling through an impressive collection of new clubs with more drivers, wedges, and putters than anyone can keep track of in a single season. Regardless of their on-course performance, blame never lands on them; it's always the clubs. Rather than seeking lessons or tweaking techniques, this individual skips straight to their local pro shop or favourite online store to search for the next promising driver. A good workman never blames his tools.

While it may seem like I'm listening, you should know my mind is entirely occupied with thoughts of golf.

When someone starts playing golf to distract themselves from work, they eventually find themselves working to escape the thoughts of golf.

Two women were out playing a leisurely game of golf. One drove off the 8th tee with an awkward slice that veered towards a group of men on the 9th hole. She screamed "fore" as a warning but unfortunately, it struck one of the men, causing him to collapse in pain and clutch at his groin.

Full of concern, the woman rushed over, expressing sincere apologies. "I'm a physio. Please let me help ease the pain." she offered.

The man, still wincing, replied, "No, no, I'll be fine, don't worry."

Curled up and holding his hands to his groin. The woman persisted in offering assistance, and eventually, he agreed.

With gentle care, she unzipped his trousers, positioned his hands aside and applied a soothing massage to the affected area. After some time, she asked him with concern, "Is that any better at all?"

Grinning, he responded, "That feels really good, thank you...but my thumb is still in bloody agony!"

"**I** would like to deny all allegations by Bob Hope that during my last game of golf, I hit an eagle, a birdie, an elk and a moose."

Gerald R. Ford (38th President of the United States)

"**G**o play golf. Go to the golf course. Hit the ball. Find the ball. Repeat until the ball is in the hole. Have fun. The end."

Chuck Hogan (Golf guru)

"This recent surgery is really throwing off my game."

"Work's booming, but it's taking a toll on my practice hours."

"I thought I ordered a fade, but my ball must have misunderstood and went for the draw."

"I had a little optical malfunction out there – my contact lens decided to take the scenic route, and now I'm navigating the course with a one-eyed perspective."

"I should've just trusted my gut on that last swing."

Golfer's *Anecdote*

"**O**ne reason golf is such an exasperating game is that a thing we learned is so easily forgotten, and we find ourselves struggling year after year with faults we had discovered and corrected time and again."
Bobby Jones (World Golf Hall of Fame inductee)

A golfer asked his caddie "Can you see any improvement in my swing?" "Absolutely, sir." said the caddie. "You're getting noticeably closer to the ball now.

Golfer: "Is it considered a sin to play golf on the sabbath?"
Caddie: "**Well**, with your playing style, sir, it might be considered a transgression on any day of the week."

Golfer: "I don't think that's my ball; it looks really old."
Caddie: "**Well**, sir, considering the time we've spent on the course, it's possible your ball has aged a bit since we teed off."

John's next-door neighbour, Mike, was always asking to borrow something, and it was getting out of hand. Catching a glimpse of Mike walking up the garden path to his front door and determined to turn the tables, John turned to Sarah, his wife, saying, "Mike won't pull it off this time. Watch and learn."

As John answered the door, Mike casually inquired, "Hey, any chance you'll be using your jet-washer this afternoon?"

Without missing a beat, John responded with a self-satisfied grin, "Oh, terribly sorry, Mike, but I'll be using it all day."

"Perfect", Mike replied, "You won't need your golf clubs. Okay if I borrow them?"

"**I**f you are caught on a golf course during a storm and are afraid of lightning, hold up a 1-iron. Not even God can hit a 1-iron."
Lee Trevino (Winner of 6 Majors)

"Believe it or not, that was just a warm-up swing, but I accidentally made contact with the ball."

"My stance is all out of whack thanks to this blister on my foot."

"If you want to see me play my best, there'll need to be some cash at stake."

"These tees are on a mission to give my ball some serious altitude."

"This new bag feels like it's got bricks in it – I'm practically getting a workout just walking to my ball, and by the time I reach it, I'm too exhausted to muster a decent drive."

Golfer's *Anecdote*

"**I** think it's more than whether or not you win or lose. It's having that opportunity on that final round, final nine, to come down the stretch with a chance to win."

Phil Mickelson (Golfer who has remained in the Top 50 official World Golf Ranking for more than 25 consecutive years)

Golfer's *Anecdote*

"**S**ometimes the biggest problem is in your head. You've got to believe you can play a shot instead of wondering where your next bad shot is coming from."

Jack Nicklaus (the 'Golden Bear' of golf, widely regarded as one of the greatest players of all time)

Paradoxically In golf, the objective is to minimize the amount of golf you actually play.

Distinguishing a whiff from a practice swing: there's one noticeable contrast— no one swears after a practice swing.

Golfer's *Gag*

During the Meadow Ridge Golf Club's gala dinner, Tom, known for his smooth demeanour, found himself chatting with the most captivating lady golfer. With more than a touch of confidence, he began to boast, "Did you know that all other club members are too scared to play a round with me? Have a guess what my handicap is?"

Swiftly, she responded, "Well, honestly, where should I start, Tom?"

"Lined up wrong."

"That tree was in my way."

"I struggled to find a comfortable footing throughout that round."

"Been hitting the gym more, and now all my club distances are doing their own thing."

"I'm so pumped to see where the ball goes that I keep peaking too soon and messing up my shot."

"I might need to make morning rounds a habit; I'm still trying to shake off that early grogginess on the course."

Golfer's *Gag*

John and Bob, two avid golfers, were playing a round when John suddenly collapsed on the course. Panicked, Bob quickly called an abulance and said, "My friend just had a heart attack! What should I do?"

The operator calmly replied, "Don't worry, I can help. First thing first, let's confirm if he's definitely dead."

A momentary hush ensued, succeeded by the echo of a gunshot.
Bob returned to the phone and asked, "Okay, now what?"

The operator, clearly shocked, stammered, "Um, well... now you take the golf ball out of his mouth and try to continue the CPR."

Missed short putt – a putt so easy that you barely think about the tap-in it needs, then you miss it.

Damaged golf ball – the ball looks fine, but when you hit it, it sounds weird and dies mid-air.

Breakfast ball – straight out onto the first tee without a warm-up. First swing of the day. Awful.

Foot-slip – perfect swing, looking good, then your foot slips from under you. Any decent partner would give you a pass.

Golfer's *Excuse*

"Got a new glove, but the sizing seems a bit off."

"My glove went in the dryer by mistake, and now it's playing hard-to-stretch."

"These plastic spikes are no friend of mine"

"This heat seems to give the balls a bit of extra oomph I wasn't expecting."

"This driver has a serious case of flexibility."

"I accidentally left the club I had in mind at home, and now I'm out here making do with what I've got in the bag.

Golfer's *Anecdote*

"**C**onfidence is the most important single factor in this game, and no matter how great your natural talent, there is only one way to obtain and sustain it: work."

Jack Nicklaus (the 'Golden Bear' of golf, widely regarded as one of the greatest players of all time)

Which other game can you play where you start with 3 friends but end with 3 enemies?

A fascinating fact about golf is that regardless of how poorly you perform, there's always room for a further decline.

Often golfers choose a cart over a caddie because it doesn't keep score, offer critiques, or burst into laughter.

The challenge with golf-related humour is that it tends to be below par.

In deep personal distress and turmoil, Kevin seeks out professional support.

"I'm getting in touch with you as I'm in a bit of a dilemma. Lately, I've had this suspicion that Jean, my wife, might be seeing another man behind my back. There have been mysterious phone calls and lots of nights out with 'the girls from the office'. I haven't mustered the courage to confront her about it. And maybe I just don't want to face the reality. Last night, though, I couldn't help myself, so I hid in the garage so I could see who was dropping her home when she returned from her 'girls' night out."

"That's when things went really wrong. As I hid there behind my golf clubs, I noticed something I hadn't seen before – a tiny crack near the head of my new hybrid driver. Do you think I could drop it off to you at the pro shop when I go to the club for a round on Saturday?"

Golfer's *Wisdom*

"**A** golf ball can stop in the fairway, rough, woods, bunker or lake. With five equally likely options, very few balls choose the fairway."
Jim Bishop (American Journalist)

"My polo is sticking to me like glue, and it's seriously cramping my swing style."

"These tees are throwing off my shot contact."

"Making sense of the break on that green is impossible"

"I'm test-driving a new ball today, and I'm still working out the spin."

"That tree needs pruning; it just bombed my backswing."

"What's wrong with the sand in these bunkers? The texture is completely different."

"**T**alking to a golf ball won't do you any good, unless you do it while your opponent is teeing off."
Bruce Lansky (poet, anthologist & golf lover)

"It takes hundreds of good golf shots to gain confidence, but only one bad one to lose it."
Jack Nicklaus (the 'Golden Bear' of golf, widely regarded as one of the greatest players of all time)

Golfer's *Excuse*

"My hayfever is awful at the moment."

"Didn't sleep well."

"Working on my swing."

"I'm more accustomed to courses that are better maintained than this one; it's not quite up to par."

"The greens seem a bit rough today."

"Got to get fitted."

"I used the wrong iron."

During a casual conversation over a glass of wine, a wife asks her husband, "If something happened to me, would you ever remarry?"

Without hesitation, the husband responds, "I would, yes."

Surprised by his quick answer, the wife probes further, "Really? Would you live here in our home with her?"

"Absolutely," he replies.

She continues, "Would she sit here on the couch with you, snuggle up and watch TV like we do?"

"She would, yes."

"Would she move into our bedroom and have all her belongings in my wardrobes?"

"Of course, yes."

"Sleep in our bed?"

"Yes, naturally."

"Would she use my golf clubs?"

The husband thinks for a second and then says, "Actually, no, that wouldn't work. She's left-handed."

"**I**f you think it's hard to meet new people, try picking up the wrong golf ball."
Jack Lemmon (Oscar winner & golf lover)

"**T**he most advanced medical brains in the universe have yet to discover a way for a man to relax himself, and looking at a golf ball is not the cure."
Milt Gross (American cartoonist and animator)

"Have they expanded the size of that pond? It's seems a lot bigger than it used to be."

"My ball landed smack in the middle of a divot on the last shot, so when I took my next swing, the contact felt off."

"The fairway bunker seemed like a tiny speck from the tee."

"There's an excessive amount of sand on this green."

"The guy who designed this course might have overdone it with the slope on the green."

"The washer has left a residue on the ball, which is throwing off its flight."

Golfer's *Anecdote*

"**S**uccess depends almost entirely on how effectively you learn to manage the game's two ultimate adversaries: the course and yourself."
Jack Nicklaus (the 'Golden Bear' of golf, widely regarded as one of the greatest players of all time)

Printed in Great Britain
by Amazon

54550775R00056